THIS BOOK IS ALL ABOUT

Birth Date

Birth Location

Adoption Date

Adoption Location

Birth Weight & Length

Lovingly Recorded By

Our Adoption Memory Book © 2020 by Mellanie Kay Journals

All rights reserved. No part of this book may be used or reproduced in any manner whatsoever without written permission except in the case of brief quotations embodied in critical articles and reviews.
First edition: 2020

TABLE OF CONTENTS

IN THE BEGINNING	4
THE PROCESS	10
ADOPTION DAY - Photos & Stats, Notes From Family & Friends	12
FOREVER FAMILY – Photos, Family Trees, All About Mommy & Daddy	18
1ST 12 MONTHS	28
TRACE MY HAND & MY FOOT	78
MY FAVORITE BOOKS/MOVIES	80
PHOTO GALLERY	82
MY ARTWORK	94
OTHER KEEPSAKES & NOTES	96

1

IN THE BEGINNING

WHY WE DECIDED ADOPTION WAS RIGHT FOR US

THE FIRST PEOPLE WE TOLD ABOUT OUR DECISION TO ADOPT

HOW THE FAMILY FELT ABOUT ADOPTION

We Chose ☐ Domestic ☐ International Adoption Because:

Where You Were Born And How We Found You:

Where & What We Did When We First Met:

What You Mean To Us:

_____
_____
_____
_____

How We Got Ready For Your Arrival:

_____
_____
_____
_____
_____
_____

Siblings & Pets Excited To Meet You:

Siblings	Age
_____	_____
_____	_____
_____	_____
_____	_____

Pets

_____
_____
_____

ADDITIONAL NOTES

THE PROCESS

USE THIS SPACE TO ENTER THE IMPORTANT DATES IN THE ADOPTION PROCESS

Example: choosing the provider, home visits, first meeting, introduction, etc.

DATE	WHAT HAPPENED

DATE THE ADOPTION
PROCESS BEGAN

DATE THE JUDGE
SAID, "YES"!

TOTAL LENGTH OF
TIME THE ADOPTION
PROCESS TOOK

12

ADOPTION DAY

ADOPTION DAY PHOTO
(4x6 photo)

date

age

location

presiding judge

ADOPTION DAY PHOTO
(4x6 photo)

ON ADOPTION DAY

_____ weather

_____ favorite toy

_____ famous actor/actress

_____ major news story

_____ current president

_____ cost of a stamp

_____ popular movie

_____ cost of a movie ticket

_____ popular song

_____ cost of gas/gallon

_____ cost of a cup of coffee

_____ cost of milk/gallon

NOTES FROM FAMILY and FRIENDS

BE HAPPY

NOTES FROM FAMILY and FRIENDS

18

FOREVER FAMILY

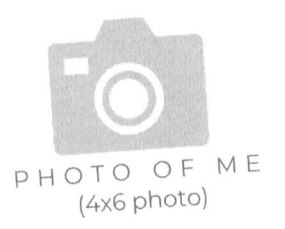

MY FOREVER FAMILY

PHOTO OF ME
(4x6 photo)

PHOTO WITH SIBLINGS
(4x6 photo)

MY FOREVER FAMILY

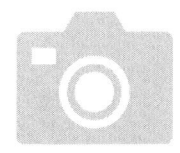

PHOTO WITH MOMMY
(trim photo to fit)

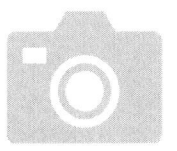

PHOTO WITH DADDY
(trim photo to fit)

PHOTO WITH FOREVER FAMILY
(4x6 photo)

MY "BIRTH FAMILY" TREE

PARENT NAME

PARENT NAME

SIBLINGS

GRANDPARENTS

GRANDPARENTS

AUNTS & UNCLES

AUNTS & UNCLES

MY "ADOPTIVE FAMILY" TREE

PARENT NAME

PARENT NAME

SIBLINGS

GRANDPARENTS

GRANDPARENTS

AUNTS & UNCLES

AUNTS & UNCLES

ALL ABOUT MOMMY

FULL NAME   BIRTHDAY

WHERE I GREW UP

MY FAVORITE CHILDHOOD MEMORIES

MY INTERESTS & HOBBIES

WHAT I WANT YOU TO KNOW ABOUT ME

Love Letter From Mommy

MY DREAM FOR YOU . .

NEVER FORGET . . .

Sweet dreams

ALL ABOUT DADDY

_____   _____
FULL NAME   BIRTHDAY

WHERE I GREW UP

MY FAVORITE CHILDHOOD MEMORIES

MY INTERESTS & HOBBIES

WHAT I WANT YOU TO KNOW ABOUT ME

Love Letter From Daddy

MY DREAM FOR YOU . .

NEVER FORGET . . .

Always dreaming

Follow your Dreams

12 MONTHS

1ST MONTH PHOTO
(4x6 photo)

1ST MONTH
with my forever family

THIS MONTH'S PERSONALITY

- ☐ quiet
- ☐ loud
- ☐ calm
- ☐ cuddly
- ☐ fussy
- ☐ silly
- ☐
- ☐

OTHER NEW THINGS THIS MONTH
Example: sounds, expressions, food, places, words, etc.

NEW FIRSTS

FAVORITE TOY(S)

THINGS I ENJOYED

BEDTIME ROUTINE

DOCTOR VISITS

ADDITIONAL NOTES

ADDITIONAL NOTES

2ND MONTH
with my forever family

2ND MONTH PHOTO
(4x6 photo)

THIS MONTH'S PERSONALITY

- [ ] quiet
- [ ] loud
- [ ] calm
- [ ] cuddly
- [ ] fussy
- [ ] silly
- [ ]
- [ ]

NEW FIRSTS

FAVORITE TOY(S)

THINGS I ENJOYED

OTHER NEW THINGS THIS MONTH

Example: sounds, expressions, food, places, words, etc.

BEDTIME ROUTINE

DOCTOR VISITS

ADDITIONAL NOTES

ADDITIONAL NOTES

3RD MONTH PHOTO
(4x6 photo)

3RD MONTH
with my forever family

THIS MONTH'S PERSONALITY

- [ ] quiet
- [ ] loud
- [ ] calm
- [ ] cuddly
- [ ] fussy
- [ ] silly
- [ ]
- [ ]

NEW FIRSTS

FAVORITE TOY(S)

THINGS I ENJOYED

OTHER NEW THINGS THIS MONTH
Example: sounds, expressions, food, places, words, etc.

BEDTIME ROUTINE

DOCTOR VISITS

ADDITIONAL NOTES

ADDITIONAL NOTES

4TH MONTH PHOTO
(4x6 photo)

4TH MONTH
with my forever family

THIS MONTH'S PERSONALITY

- [ ] quiet
- [ ] loud
- [ ] calm
- [ ] cuddly
- [ ] fussy
- [ ] silly
- [ ]
- [ ]

NEW FIRSTS

FAVORITE TOY(S)

THINGS I ENJOYED

OTHER NEW THINGS THIS MONTH
Example: sounds, expressions, food, places, words, etc.

BEDTIME ROUTINE

DOCTOR VISITS

ADDITIONAL NOTES

ADDITIONAL NOTES

5TH MONTH
with my forever family

LETS HANG OUT

5TH MONTH PHOTO
(4x6 photo)

THIS MONTH'S PERSONALITY

- [ ] quiet
- [ ] loud
- [ ] calm
- [ ] cuddly
- [ ] fussy
- [ ] silly
- [ ]
- [ ]

NEW FIRSTS

FAVORITE TOY(S)

THINGS I ENJOYED

OTHER NEW THINGS THIS MONTH
Example: sounds, expressions, food, places, words, etc.

BEDTIME ROUTINE

DOCTOR VISITS

ADDITIONAL NOTES

ADDITIONAL NOTES

6TH MONTH PHOTO
(4x6 photo)

6TH MONTH
with my forever family

THIS MONTH'S PERSONALITY

- ☐ quiet
- ☐ loud
- ☐ calm
- ☐ cuddly
- ☐ fussy
- ☐ silly
- ☐
- ☐

OTHER NEW THINGS THIS MONTH
Example: sounds, expressions, food, places, words, etc.

NEW FIRSTS

FAVORITE TOY(S)

THINGS I ENJOYED

BEDTIME ROUTINE

DOCTOR VISITS

ADDITIONAL NOTES

ADDITIONAL NOTES

1ST MONTH PHOTO
(4x6 photo)

7TH MONTH
with my forever family

THIS MONTH'S PERSONALITY

- [ ] quiet
- [ ] loud
- [ ] calm
- [ ] cuddly
- [ ] fussy
- [ ] silly
- [ ]
- [ ]

OTHER NEW THINGS THIS MONTH

Example: sounds, expressions, food, places, words, etc.

BEDTIME ROUTINE

NEW FIRSTS

FAVORITE TOY(S)

THINGS I ENJOYED

DOCTOR VISITS

ADDITIONAL NOTES

ADDITIONAL NOTES

8TH MONTH
with my forever family

2ND MONTH PHOTO
(4x6 photo)

THIS MONTH'S PERSONALITY

- [ ] quiet
- [ ] loud
- [ ] calm
- [ ] cuddly
- [ ] fussy
- [ ] silly
- [ ]

NEW FIRSTS

FAVORITE TOY(S)

THINGS I ENJOYED

OTHER NEW THINGS THIS MONTH

Example: sounds, expressions, food, places, words, etc.

BEDTIME ROUTINE

DOCTOR VISITS

ADDITIONAL NOTES

ADDITIONAL NOTES

3RD MONTH PHOTO
(4x6 photo)

9TH MONTH
with my forever family

THIS MONTH'S PERSONALITY

- ☐ quiet
- ☐ loud
- ☐ calm
- ☐ cuddly
- ☐ fussy
- ☐ silly
- ☐
- ☐

NEW FIRSTS

FAVORITE TOY(S)

THINGS I ENJOYED

OTHER NEW THINGS THIS MONTH

Example: sounds, expressions, food, places, words, etc.

BEDTIME ROUTINE

DOCTOR VISITS

ADDITIONAL NOTES

ADDITIONAL NOTES

4TH MONTH PHOTO
(4x6 photo)

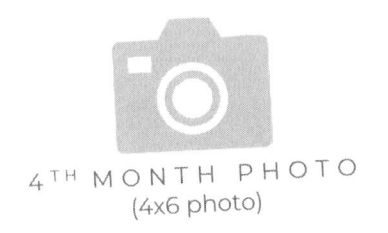

10TH MONTH
with my forever family

THIS MONTH'S PERSONALITY

- [ ] quiet
- [ ] loud
- [ ] calm
- [ ] cuddly
- [ ] fussy
- [ ] silly
- [ ]
- [ ]

NEW FIRSTS

FAVORITE TOY(S)

THINGS I ENJOYED

OTHER NEW THINGS THIS MONTH

Example: sounds, expressions, food, places, words, etc.

BEDTIME ROUTINE

DOCTOR VISITS

ADDITIONAL NOTES

ADDITIONAL NOTES

11TH MONTH
with my forever family

LETS HANG OUT

5TH MONTH PHOTO
(4x6 photo)

THIS MONTH'S PERSONALITY

- ☐ quiet
- ☐ loud
- ☐ calm
- ☐ cuddly
- ☐ fussy
- ☐ silly
- ☐
- ☐

OTHER NEW THINGS THIS MONTH

Example: sounds, expressions, food, places, words, etc.

NEW FIRSTS

BEDTIME ROUTINE

FAVORITE TOY(S)

THINGS I ENJOYED

DOCTOR VISITS

ADDITIONAL NOTES

ADDITIONAL NOTES

6TH MONTH PHOTO
(4x6 photo)

12TH MONTH
with my forever family

THIS MONTH'S PERSONALITY

- [ ] quiet
- [ ] loud
- [ ] calm
- [ ] cuddly
- [ ] fussy
- [ ] silly
- [ ]
- [ ]

NEW FIRSTS

FAVORITE TOY(S)

THINGS I ENJOYED

OTHER NEW THINGS THIS MONTH

Example: sounds, expressions, food, places, words, etc.

BEDTIME ROUTINE

DOCTOR VISITS

ADDITIONAL NOTES

ADDITIONAL NOTES

MY HAND & MY FOOT

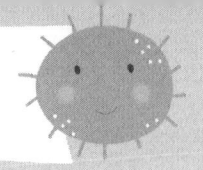

Trace my hand and foot on ADOPTION DAY

DATE: AGE:

MY HAND & MY FOOT

Trace again 1 YEAR later

DATE: AGE:

My Favorite Books/Movies

More of My Favorite Books/Movies

1ST YEAR PHOTO CHECKLIST

INFANT

- ○ 1st BATH
- ○ 1ST FEEDING
- ○ 1ST DOCTOR VISIT
- ○ 1ST HAIRCUT
- ○ LEARNING TO CRAWL
- ○ 1ST TIME STANDING
- ○ GIVING KISSES
- ○ FAVORITE TOYS
- ○ 1ST STEP
- ○ 1ST TOOTH
- ○ 1ST BIRTHDAY
- ○ 1ST CHRISTMAS, EASTER, HALLOWEEN

OLDER CHILD

- ○ 1st DAY OF SCHOOL
- ○ 1ST BIRTHDAY CELEBRATION
- ○ NEW BEDROOM
- ○ FAVORITE TOYS
- ○ WITH FAMILY PET(S)
- ○ HOBBIES
- ○ DANCING
- ○ SPORTS
- ○ VACATIONS
- ○ NEW FRIENDS
- ○ CHORES
- ○ 1ST CHRISTMAS, EASTER, HALLOWEEN

OTHER PHOTO IDEAS

- ○
- ○
- ○
- ○

- ○
- ○
- ○
- ○

PHOTO GALLERY

(trim to fit)

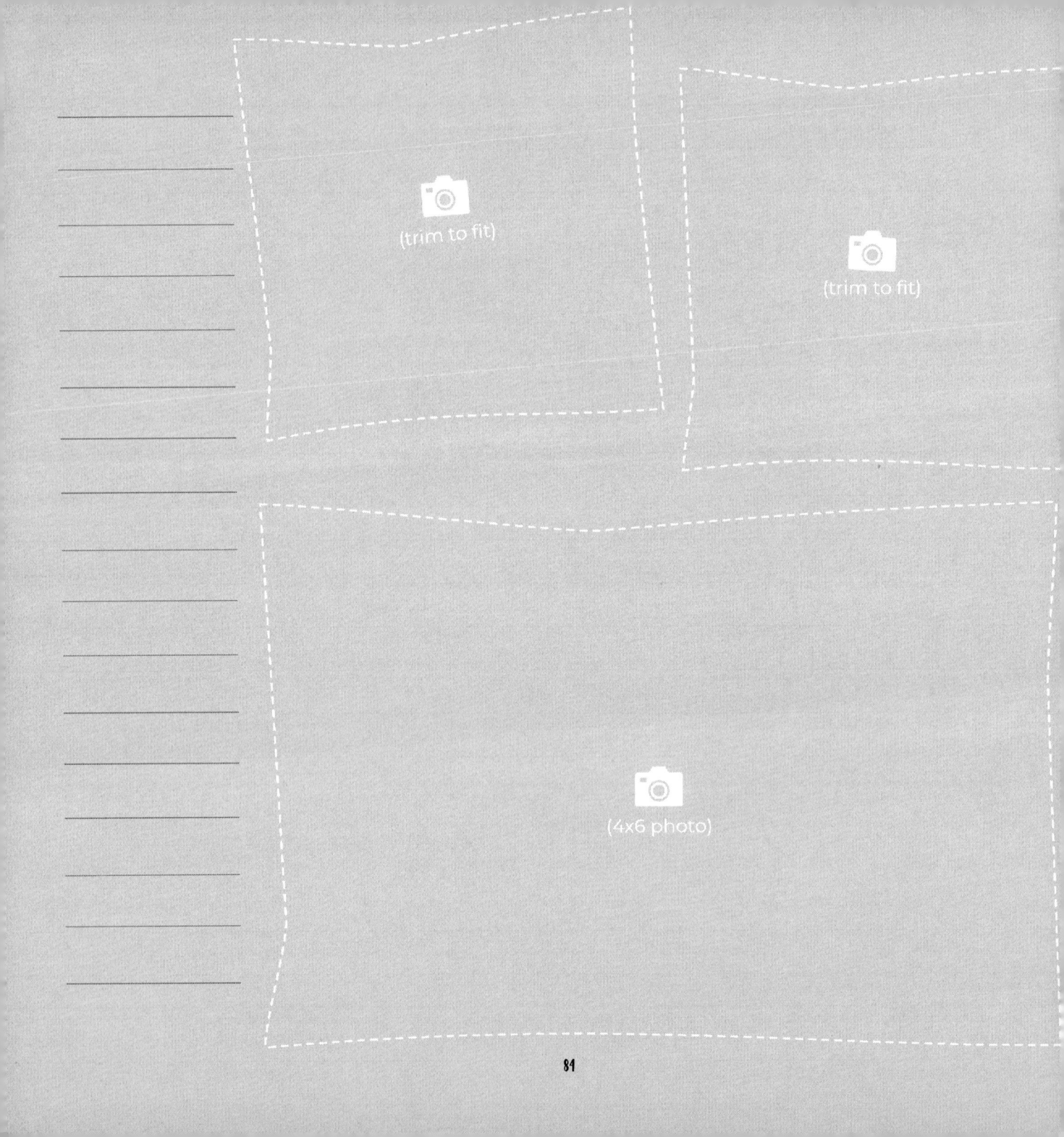

(trim to fit)

(4x6 photo)

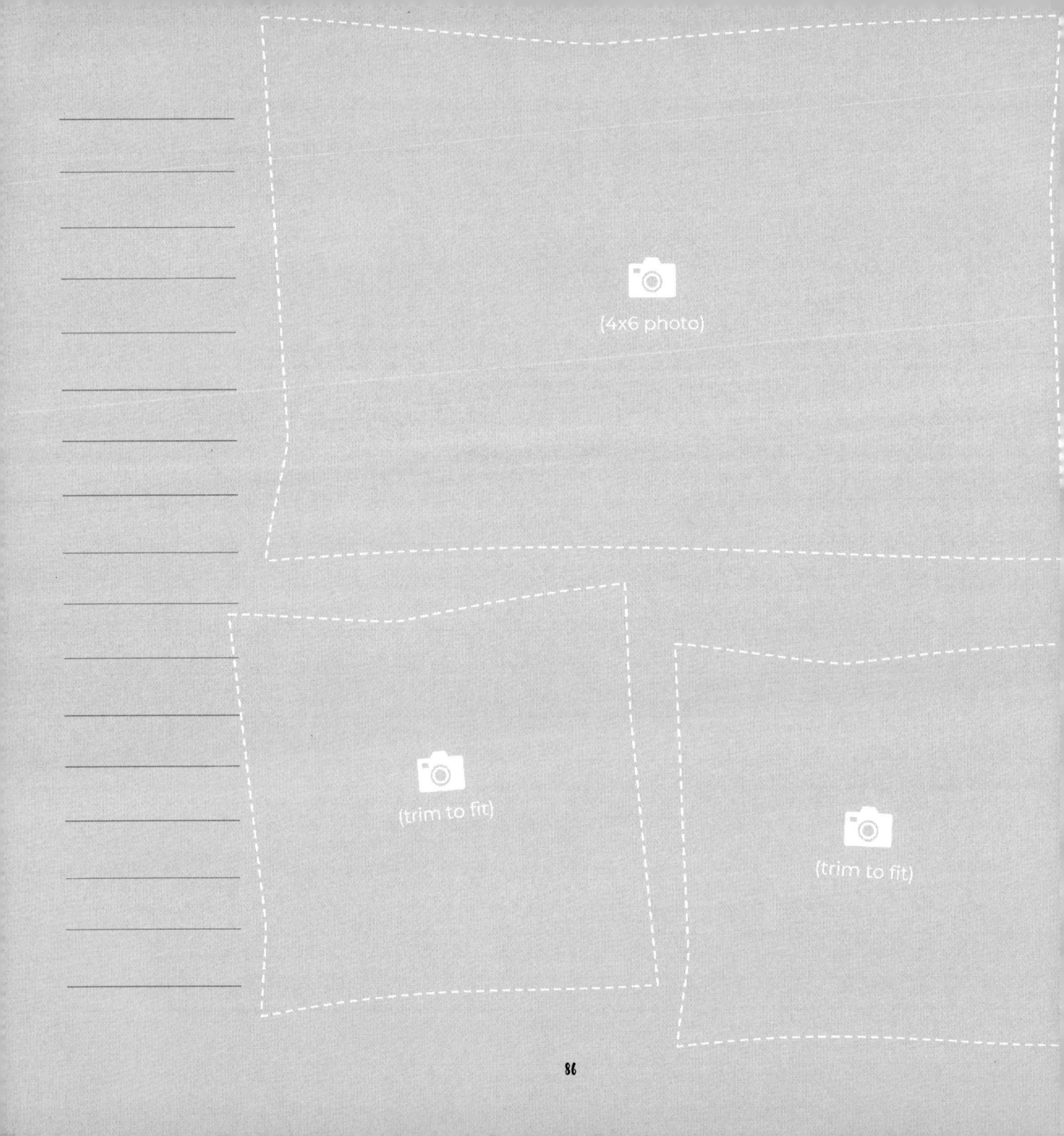

(4x6 photo)

(trim to fit)

(trim to fit)

(trim to fit)

(trim to fit)

(4x6 photo)

(4x6 photo)

(trim to fit)

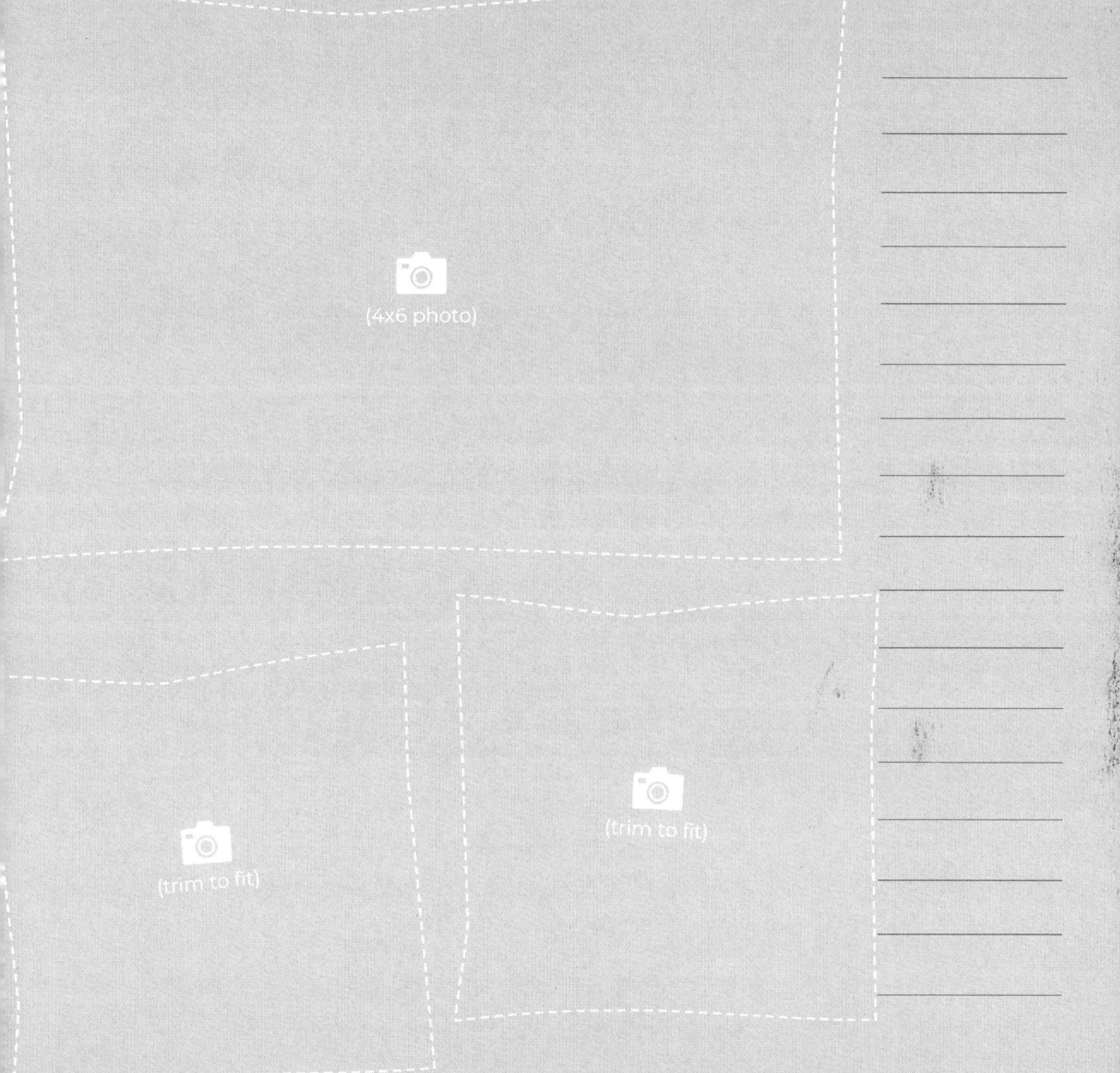

(4x6 photo)

(trim to fit)

(trim to fit)

(trim to fit)

(trim to fit)

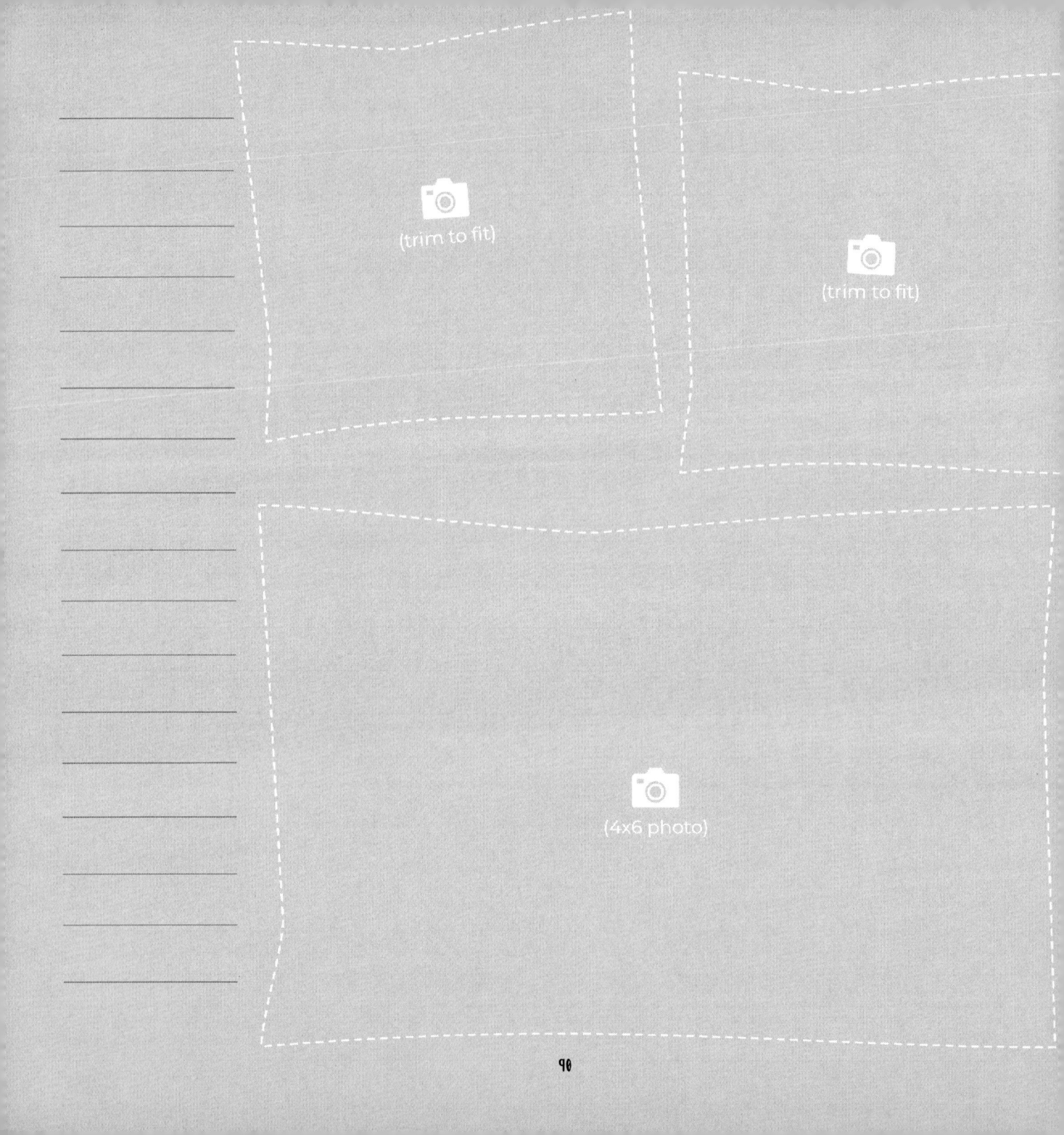

(4x6 photo)

(4x6 photo)

(trim to fit)

(4x6 photo)

(trim to fit)

(trim to fit)

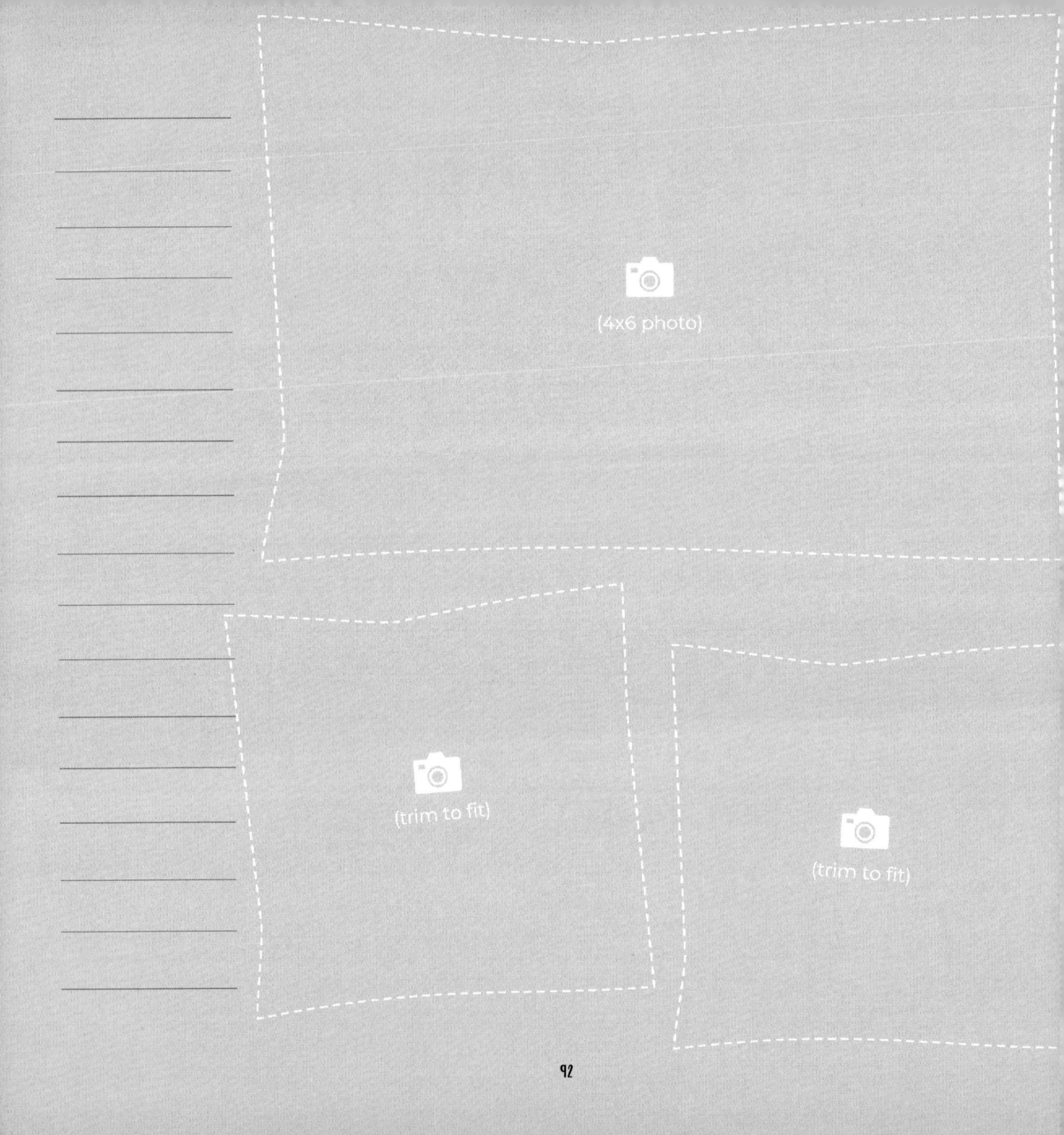

(trim to fit)

(trim to fit)

(4x6 photo)

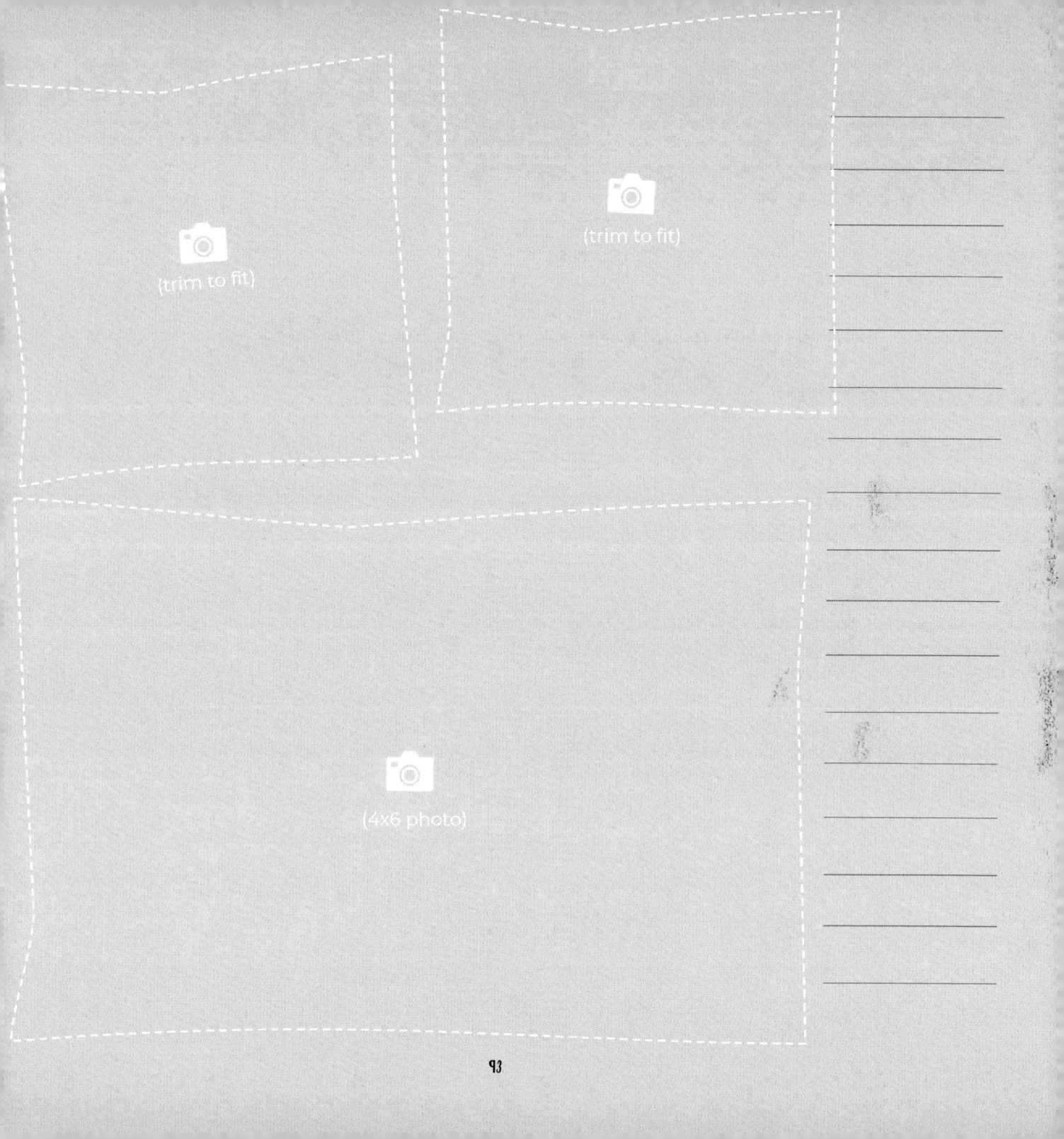

look how good I color

Look how good I draw

other keepsakes

_____

_____

_____

_____

_____

_____

_____

(sample from my first haircut)

(attach a memory here)

other keepsakes

other keepsakes

_____

_____

_____

_____

_____

_____

_____

_____

(attach a memory here)

ADDITIONAL NOTES

ADDITIONAL NOTES

Printed in Great Britain
by Amazon